# NO, NOT CHINATOWN! THE REAL CHINA!

Explorer Kids Geography Book 1st Grade

Children's Explore The World Books

BABY PROFESSOR
EDUCATION KIDS

Speedy Publishing LLC

40 E. Main St. #1156

Newark, DE 19711

www.speedypublishing.com

Copyright 2017

All Rights reserved. No part of this book may be reproduced or used in any way or form or by any means whether electronic or mechanical, this means that you cannot record or photocopy any material ideas or tips that are provided in this book.

In this book, we're going to talk about exploring the country of China. So, let's get right to it!

**CHINA** is a huge country. It has a very large landmass, which is just a little smaller than the United States. It's the most populated country in the world with over 1.3 billion people. It has four times the number of people as the United States. China was isolated from the rest of the world in ancient times. The reason is that there were barriers on all sides. There are dry deserts located in the north and also in the west. To the east was the vast Pacific Ocean. The mountains at the south were so tall that they were almost impossible to cross.

# THE RIVERS OF CHINA

The two major rivers of China are the Yellow River and the Yangtze River. The Yellow River is the sixth longest in the world and the Yangtze River is the third longest. The Yellow River is 3,395 miles long and the Yangtze River is 3,988 miles long. Both rivers run from west to east and the Yellow River is north of the Yangtze River.

Yellow River in China

The Chinese people sometimes call the Yellow River "China's Sorrow." Although the river brings them water and good soil, it also brings them dangerous floods.

The very first civilization in China was started close to the Yellow River. Ancient Chinese people constructed small towns along the river's banks. The fertile yellow soil located there was used to grow millet, which is a type of grain.

The farms along the Yangtze River grew rice. The climate was warm and rainy, which is perfect for growing rice. After many centuries, the land along the Yangtze River became very important and some landowners became wealthy. Because the Yangtze was so wide and difficult to cross, it divided north China from south China.

Farmer working in the farm

Three Gorges Dam

In modern times, a huge dam called the Three Gorges Dam has been built on the Yangtze River. It creates a very large amount of hydroelectric power from the water in the river.

# THE MOUNTAINS SOUTH AND SOUTHEAST OF CHINA

The Himalayan Mountains are located to the south and the southeast of China. They are the world's tallest mountains and include Mount Everest. People who practice the religion of Buddhism believe that these beautiful mountains are sacred.

Himalayan Mountains

Taklamakan Desert

# THE DESERTS OF CHINA

The Gobi Desert is a cold desert in the northern part of China. The Taklamakan Desert is west of the Gobi. They are two of the largest deserts in the world and are very dangerous to cross. They provided a natural border that kept China isolated from the rest of the world.

However, the Mongolians lived in the Gobi Desert and they were always trying to invade China. The Chinese built an enormous wall to keep them out.

The great Gobi Desert

# THE GREAT WALL OF CHINA

In 2007, more than 100 million people voted on the list of the new "Seven Wonders of the World" and the Great Wall made the list. It's an amazing structure.

The Great Wall

The Great Wall of China is over 5,000 miles long. In some places it's over 30 feet in height and 15 feet in width. It is a symbol for the country of China and is the world's longest manmade structure. The building of the Great Wall started around the 5th century BC.

Qin Shi Huang

When Qin Shi Huang, China's first emperor took the throne in 221 BC, he decided that he wanted to expand the wall. He wanted the wall to be huge and have thousands of towers. Soldiers could look out from the tall towers so they could see if enemies were trying to attack the Chinese people.

No one knows for sure exactly how many people it took to build the Great Wall.

Some historians believe that it took millions of workers over a period of time spanning 1,000 years. The Great Wall was built by slaves, peasants, and criminals as a punishment for their crimes. There are more than 7,000 lookout towers throughout the length of the wall.

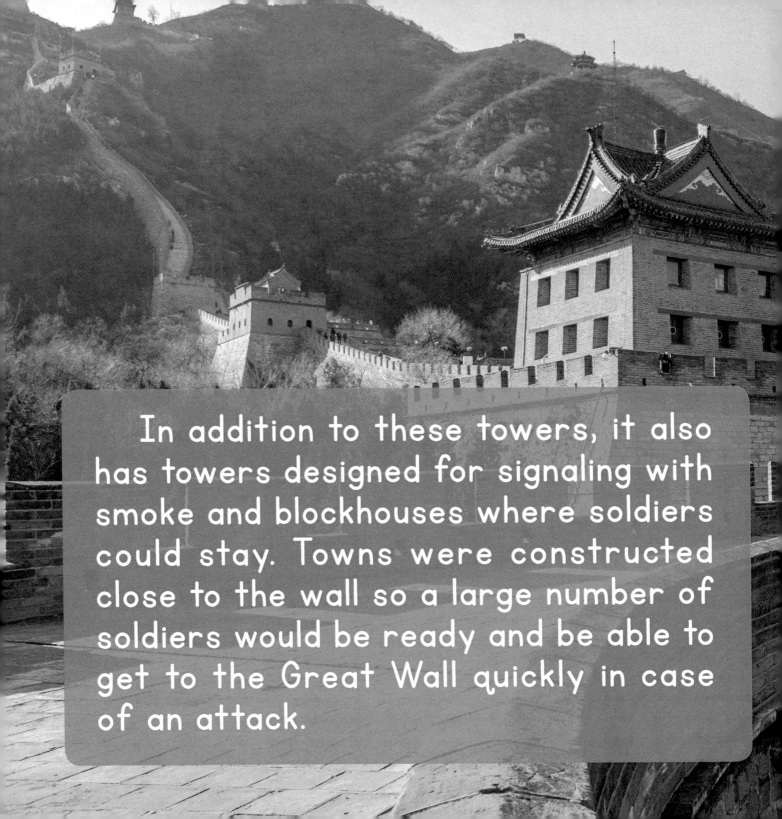

In addition to these towers, it also has towers designed for signaling with smoke and blockhouses where soldiers could stay. Towns were constructed close to the wall so a large number of soldiers would be ready and be able to get to the Great Wall quickly in case of an attack.

The Forbidden City in Beijing, China

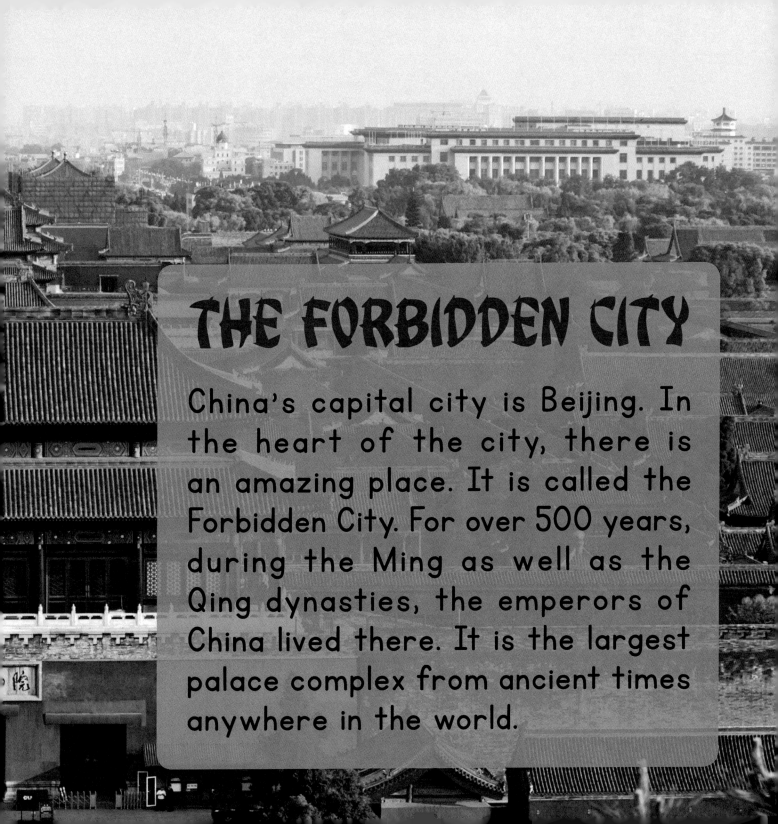

# THE FORBIDDEN CITY

China's capital city is Beijing. In the heart of the city, there is an amazing place. It is called the Forbidden City. For over 500 years, during the Ming as well as the Qing dynasties, the emperors of China lived there. It is the largest palace complex from ancient times anywhere in the world.

Zhu Di

The Forbidden City was constructed between 1406 to 1420 AD. The Yongle Emperor, whose name was Zhu Di, is the emperor who ordered the construction of this huge city. He was the third emperor of the Ming dynasty.

Over a million people worked on the building of this palace. The best supplies were used for construction. They used blocks of marble and logs from a type of very rare tree called the Phoebe Zhennan found only in the jungles of southwestern China. There were even bricks called "golden bricks."

These bricks were actually made of clay and the batches took many months to bake. They were so smooth when they were finished that they made a metallic sound. When the palace was finished in 1420 AD, the emperor moved the capital city to Beijing.

The buildings of the Forbidden City cover an area that is 178 acres. There are 90 different palaces with courtyards. There are over 900 buildings in the city and over 8,000 rooms! The floors in all the buildings covered over 1.6 million square feet. It's a good thing that the emperor had hundreds of servants to take care of the palaces.

皇建有極

天心降鑒惟萬方臣庶安

祖訓昭垂我後嗣子孫尚

Historic throne at the Forbidden City

In addition to being a place to live, the palace was designed as a fortress to keep the emperor and his family safe. There is a wall with a height of 26 feet that surrounds it. There's also a moat that's 170 feet in width. Soldiers stood guard and kept a watchful eye for enemies in the palace's tall towers.

# THE TERRACOTTA ARMY

Emperor Qin Shi Huang, the first emperor of China, is responsible for another amazing ancient site as well as the work he commanded on the Great Wall.

Modern statue of emperor Qin Shi Huang near the site of his tomb

Emperor Qin decided that he never wanted to die. He spent much of his time and resources searching for a way to become eternal and live forever. He built an enormous tomb for himself. He wanted to make sure that there would be an army there to protect him as well as to make sure he kept his power.

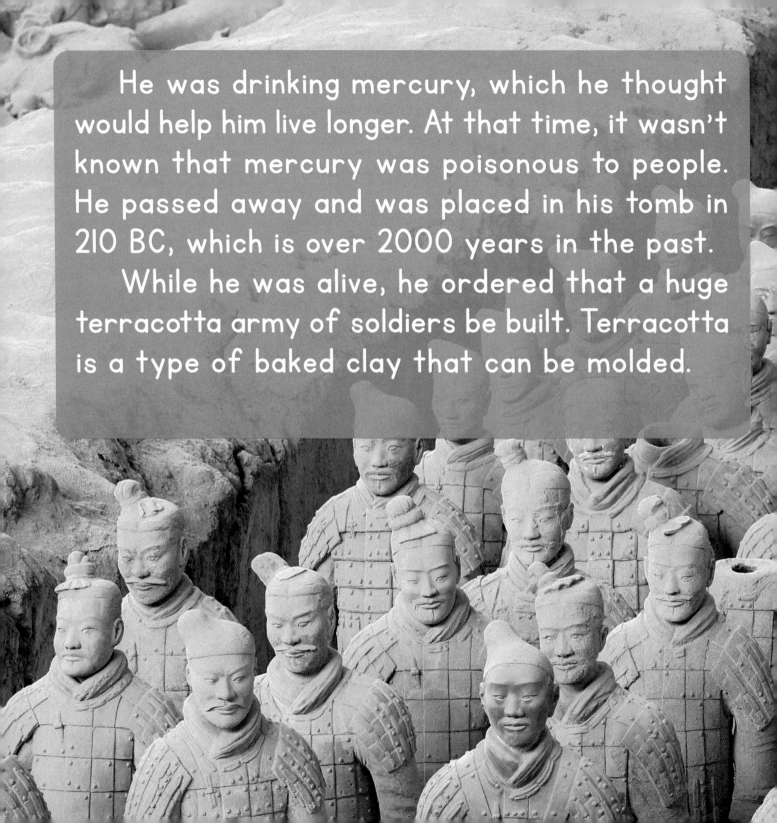

He was drinking mercury, which he thought would help him live longer. At that time, it wasn't known that mercury was poisonous to people. He passed away and was placed in his tomb in 210 BC, which is over 2000 years in the past.

While he was alive, he ordered that a huge terracotta army of soldiers be built. Terracotta is a type of baked clay that can be molded.

Terracotta Warriors

No one knew about this army in modern times until a group of farmers discovered it in 1974. They were digging a hole for a well when they made the amazing discovery of the terracotta soldiers.

These statues of soldiers were made at the average height of about 5 feet 11 inches. There are over 8,000 of them! They were buried about a mile away from the emperor's main tomb.

It's incredible that there are so many of these clay soldiers, but what's even more incredible is that they are all different ages with different faces and with different clothes! They have different army ranks. As well as the features on their faces being different, they also have different facial hair, hairstyles, and expressions. Some look calm, but others are very angry and just can't wait to fight.

Terracotta warriors great hall

Archaeologists believe that there must have been at least 700,000 artists and craftsmen needed to create this huge army. They had molds that they used for the body parts and worked like an assembly line. They used about ten different head shapes to make sure that people from different areas of China were represented. After the general body shape was put together, the custom features to make each statue different were added.

18

The terracotta soldiers held different types of weapons such as daggers, swords, and crossbows.

Even though the terracotta army is famous for its rows and rows of soldiers, there were other kinds of statues too. There were 150 cavalry horses that were created to be the same size as real horses. There are also over 100 chariots with 500 horses. These are all life-size.

Archaeologists are carefully putting together the broken statues piece by piece. It's one of the most amazing archaeological sites ever found. They still look amazing today, but 2,000 years ago they were painted in different colors and had a shiny lacquer on them. They must have been even more spectacular!

# SUMMARY

China's geography kept its civilization isolated from the rest of the world for many centuries. Today, it's the most populated country in the world with over 1.3 billion people. The Great Wall, the Forbidden City, and the Terracotta Army are some of the most amazing manmade ancient structures to explore in the country of China.

# CHINA

Awesome! Now that you know more about the country of China, you may want to read about a famous philosopher who lived in China in the Baby Professor book Who Was Confucius? Ancient China Book for Kids.

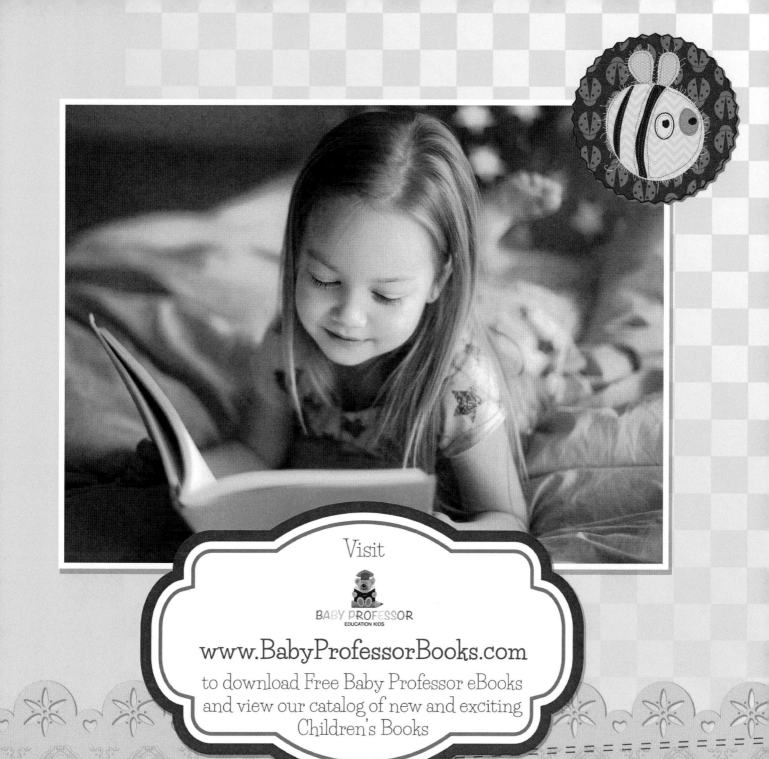

Visit

**BABY PROFESSOR**
EDUCATION KIDS

# www.BabyProfessorBooks.com

to download Free Baby Professor eBooks
and view our catalog of new and exciting
Children's Books